Spiritually Poetic for the Heart of the Saints

Charles Lee Smith Jr.

authorHOUSE®

AuthorHouse™
1663 Liberty Drive
Bloomington, IN 47403
www.authorhouse.com
Phone: 1 (800) 839-8640

Published by AuthorHouse   03/22/2017

ISBN: 978-1-4107-6582-6 (sc)
ISBN: 978-1-4107-6583-3 (e)

Print information available on the last page.

This book is printed on acid-free paper.

CONTENTS

The Prophet The Seer The Pastor 1

My Potter My Potter.. 2

A Voice With In 3

Faith And Faith Substance 4

Life Giving Bread 5

The Fallen Angel... 6

Change With In 7

Soldiering Saints 8

Praise For My Miracle 9

My Heart Will Know 10

The Lords Got A Hold Of Me...11

If You Give Your Life To The Lord 12

Saints Fall But We Rise Again.. 13

Safe In The Light 14

When The Light Comes On 15

Mustard Seed Faith 16

Pray Like A Kid Again 17

Dreams From The Lord 18

Father Speak To Me 19

Victory 20

Life And Death Is In Your Tongue 21

Run To Him.. 22

"I Am "... 23

All Because Of You 24

His Love His Blood 25

Mothers Day 26

Ask Yourself 27

Lord' Lord Jesus 39

If You Join With Him 40

The Greatest Plan 41

Heaven Is The Place To Be 42

A Prayer Can Change Some Things 43

Spiritual Dance 44

The Victory Is In The Blood 45

"Jesus" Claim That Name 46

Forever Eternal Everlasting 47

Look Inside Yourself 48

A Friend 50

Moved By The Spirit 51

Spiritual Inspiration 52

Valentines For The Married Saints In Love 53

Valentines For The Married Saints In Love 54

Steppin Out On Faith Steppin Out Today 55

You Shined Your Light On Me 56

THE PROPHET THE SEER THE PASTOR

I'VE BEEN CHOSEN BY THE MOST HIGH
AND KNOWING SO I NEVER ASK WHY
I'M LED BY HIS SPIRIT EVERYDAY AND EVERY NIGHT
ALL THE DAYS OF MY LIFE
I'M LED TO THE PLACE HE WANTS ME TO BE
I'M LED TO THE FACE THAT HE WANTS ME TO SEE
I'M LED BY HIS SPIRIT TO SPEAK TO THE DEAD
AS A LIGHT THAT SHINES IN THE DARK
AND DARKNESS CAN'T COMPREHEND
FOR WITH IN ME IS WHERE THE LORD LIVES
AND MY STRENGHT IS ALL HIS
WHEN IM SLEEP HE'S THERE TO SPEAK TO ME
AND WHEN I ARISE IN ME HIS WORDS ARE ALIVE
SO THERE I AM WHERE HIS SPIRIT LEADS
ON EVERY HIGH MOUTAIN AND IN EVERY DARK CORNER
HIS WORDS THEY FLOW OUT OF ME
LIKE RUNNING WATER
FOR THOSE THAT HAVE EARS TO HEAR
AND THOSE THAT HAVE EYES TO SEE
THEY CAN RECEIVE HIS WATER
AND THOSE THAT DO ARE PURGED AND SET FREE
FOR THIS REASON, I THANK THE MOST HIGH MAJESTY
JEHOVAH GOD
THAT HE CHOSE ME

-BY CHARLES LEE SMITH JR.

MY POTTER MY POTTER

MOLD ME IN THE WAY
THAT YOU DESIRE ME TO BE
MOLD ME IN THE WAY
THAT YOU WOULD HAVE ME TO SPEAK
MOLD ME IN THE WAY
THAT MY FEET WON'T TRIP, STUMBLE
OR ROLL DOWN THE PATH OF UNRIGHTEOUSNESS
MOLD ME IN A WAY MY HEART SHOULD KNOW
WHILE TODAY IS TODAY, THE WAY I SHOULD GO
MY POTTER MY POTTER I'M YOUR CLAY
MOLD ME MY POTTER AND HAVE YOUR WAY
MOLD ME TO BE IN YOUR RIGHTEOUSNESS
MOLD ME MY POTTER TO STAY AWAY FROM SIN
MOLD ME MY POTTER FOR I'M YOUR CLAY
AFTER ALL THE SHAPING AND MOLDING TODAY
INPUT IN ME MY POTTER THAT WITH YOU IM SAFE
BECAUSE IT'S YOUR WILL MY POTTER
AND I'LL ALWAYS BE
YOUR' CLAY

-BY CHARLES LEE SMITH JR.

A VOICE WITH IN

THERE'S A VOICE THAT'S CALLING YOU
A VOICE WITHOUT A FACE
AND EVEN WITH ALL YOUR SENSE'S IT DOES'NT LEAVE A TRACE
THIS VOICE TALKS TO YOU AT THE CRACK OF DAWN
THIS VOICE TALKS TO YOU WEATHER YOU'RE HAPPY OR SAD
IT TALKS TO YOU WHEN YOU'RE SCARED AND WANT TO RUN
MOST OF ALL
IT TALKS TO YOU RIGHT BEFORE
SOMETHINGS GOING TO GO WRONG
OR EVEN BEFORE YOU DO SOMETHING DUMB
THIS VOICE DOES'NT NEED A FACE OR FEET TO RUN
THIS VOICE IS IN YOUR MIND AND IT CRAVES FOR YOUR HEART
THIS VOICE IS A POWERFUL VOICE
BECAUSE IT COMES FROM GOD
THIS VOICE WHEN IT CALLS YOU
IT CALLS YOU TO LOVE AND AFFECTION
SO IT CALLS YOU TO A PATH THAT'S NARROW AND PERFECT
A PATH THAT'S NOT WEAKENED
OR AFFECTED FROM THE WAYS OF THE WORLD
BUT A PATH THAT'S LOADED WITH THE POWER OF LOVE
SO OUR EARS BECOME OPENED AND OUR EYES START TO SEE
NOT THE FACE THE PLACE WHERE THIS VOICE IS PERCEIVED
SO HARDEN NOT YOUR HEART
WHILE TODAY IS TODAY
AND LISTEN TO THE VOICE WHEN IT CALLS YOUR NAME
BECAUSE WHEN YOU FINALLY HEAR THIS VOICE
YOUR' HEART WILL SAY
IT'S MY FATHER
MY GOD
LEAD ME MY FATHER
LEAD THE WAY

-BY CHARLES LEE SMITH JR.

FAITH AND FAITH SUBSTANCE

IN THE NAME OF JESUS I DO PRAY
EVERYDAY THE SAME WAY, ON MY KNEES
I CALL HIS NAME
AND WHEN I DO THERE IS NO SHAME
HE LIFTS ME UP WHEN IM DOWN, BECAUSE
OF HIS BLOOD I'M FOUND
I LOOK TO HIM IN A TIME OF NEED, I LOOK
TO HIM FOR EVERYTHING
FOR HIS LOVE I SACRIFICE EVERY THING, BECAUSE HIS LOVE
IS ALL I NEED
I BELIEVE HE'S THE ONLY ONE THAT CAN
MEND MY BROKEN HEART
HE'S THE ONLY ONE THAT CAN
GIVE ME A NEW START, HE'S MY ROCK HE'S MY SHIELD
BECAUSE OF HIM IM SEALED, THROUGH HIS BLOOD I'VE
RECEIVED GRACE
HIS COMMANDMENTS I KEEP, HIS WORDS I CHERISH
AND BECAUSE OF THEM I SHALL NEVER PERISH
I'VE TRUSTED IN HIM WITH ALL MY HEART
AND EVERYDAY WITH HIM IS A BRAND NEW START
IN JESUS NAME I DO PRAY, AND EVERYDAY IT SHOULD BE
DONE THAT WAY

-BY CHARLES LEE SMITH JR.

LIFE GIVING BREAD

WE EAT BREAD THAT GOES GOOD WITH MEAT
BREAD THAT TASTE GOOD WITH CHEESE
AND BREAD THAT WE BAKE WITH SPECIAL SEASONING
BREAD THAT'S JUST GOOD FOR OUR EARTHLY BODIES'
BUT THERE'S BREAD THAT'S NOT MADE FROM EARTHLY STUFF
BREAD THAT'S GOOD FOR YOUR SPIRITUAL BUILD UP
BREAD THAT YOU CAN EAT
WHEN EVER WHERE EVER ANYTIME DURING THE DAY
BREAD THAT YOU SHOULD EAT IN A HUNGRY MANS FACE
BECAUSE THIS BREAD
IS THE BREAD THAT TRANFORMS A LIFE
THE SAME BREAD THAT CONQUERS SPIRITUAL FIGHTS
THE TRUE BREAD FROM HEAVEN
THAT WILL TAKE YOU STRAIGHT
TO YOUR ETERNAL LIFE
SO DON'T STARVE YOURSELF WITH THE EARTHLY STUFF
BUT FEED YOUR MIND BODY AND SOUL
WITH THE TRUE BREAD FROM HEAVEN
WITH LIFE IN EVERY BITE, AND THE NAME THAT'S ABOVE
ALL THE REST, JESUS!

-BY CHARLES LEE SMITH JR.

THE FALLEN ANGEL

WHO RAISED THE SAINTS
THERE ONCE WAS AN ANGEL BEAUTIFUL AS CAN BE
he TURNED AGAINST his CREATER THAT MADE him TO BE
he THOUGHT he WAS SOMETHING MORE THAN HIS EYES COULD SEE
he THOUGHT he WAS GREATER THAN THE KING
HIS MAJESTY, he BROUGHT WAR AND
DECEPTION AGAINST THE KING OF ALL KINGS IN
A BATTLE ON ANY DAY he COULD NOT WIN
NOW he's BEEN KNOCKED DOWN TO A PLACE
WHERE his LIGHT WON'T SHINE
TO A PLACE WHERE CHOAS AND DARKNESS IS
ALL THE TIME, WHERE he's MADE himself
KING OF DECEPTION AND he's THE FATHER OF ALL
LIES, NOW he's JUST THE ENEMY OF US
- MAN KIND – he's EVEN MADE AN ATTEMPT ON
THE LIFE OF JESUS, THE SON OF THE KING
BUT THE FATHER RAISED HIM AND SEATED HIM NEXT TO THE
THRONE ON THE RIGHT SIDE OF THE MOST HIGH AND MAJESTIC
KING OF ALL, NOW THERE'S NOT ONE WEAPON he CAN FORM
THAT WILL PROSPER AGAINST US, BECAUSE WE STAND IN THE
FORM OF HIS RIGHTEOUSNESS, WE STAND IN THE IMAGE OF HIS
MAJESTY THE MOST HIGH, AND WE'RE COVERED IN THE BLOOD
OF THE SON WHO ONCED DIED, NOW WE WAIT FOR THE DAY TO
BE RAISED TO HIS STATE OF GRACE, AND ON THAT DAY NO MORE
WILL WE HAVE TO SUFFER THIS PLACE, WE WILL BE IN OUR NEW
HOME WITH OUR LORD ON HIS MAJESTIC THRONE ON THE RIGHT
SIDE OF THE MOST HIGH AND MAJECTIC KING OF ALL AND FROM
THIS MAGNIFICENT PLACE WHERE WE WILL LOOK DOWN ON THIS
SELF MADE KING AND ALL THOSE WHO CHOSE TO CONTINUE
IN SIN, THEY WILL BE BOUND TO A PLACE WHERE FIRE AND
TORMENT WILL BE EVERYDAY EVERLASTING FOR ETERNITY
THAT'S WHY I THANK THE MOST HIGH FOR THE PRECIOUS
BLOOD OF THE LAMB AND THAT HE OPENED MY EYES
AND EARS SO THAT MY HEART CAN SEE THE TRUTH WHEN
IT'S IN FRONT OF ME, SO THAT I CAN LIVE WHERE HE
LIVES, IN HIS FATHERS HOUSE IN MY OWN MANSION

-BY CHARLES LEE SMITH JR.

Spiritually Poetic for the Heart of the Saints

CHANGE WITH IN

DOES'NT MATTER THE MISTAKES YOU MADE
OF HIM YOU DON'T HAVE TO BE AFRAID
YOU CAN GO TO HIM ANYTIME YOU LIKE
BECAUSE IT'S WHERE HE WANTS YOU
RIGHT BY HIS SIDE
NOW ALL THE WORRING AND STRIFE YOU HAD
AND ALL THE DAYS OF JUST BEING SAD, NO LONGER EXIST
BECAUSE IN HIM ALL THINGS CAN BE FIXED
BECAUSE FAITH IN HIM MAKES THE WAY STRAIGHT FOR YOU
"JESUS"
THAT'S HIS NAME
WHEN YOU OPEN UP TO HIM HE'LL TAKE AWAY THE SHAME
HE'LL BE LIKE A TREE IN THE GROUND
ROOTED DOWN DEEP IN YOUR BONES
WHERE HE CAN RELEASE THIS THING
THIS THING THAT CAUSES CHANGE
A CHANGE THAT WILL AFFECT YOUR LIFE
AND PEOPLE WILL SEE YOU AND IN YOU
THEY WILL SEE HIS LIGHT
SO STAND WHERE YOU ARE AND WALK IN FAITH
AND REMAIN ON THE PATH THAT HE'S MADE STRAIGHT
ALTHOUGH THERE MAY BE MANY BATTLES AND MANY FIGHTS
IN HIM WE ARE MORE THAN CONQUERS
SO DON'T LOOSE SIGHT AND DON'T LOOSE HEART
BECAUSE THE LIFE OF A SAINT IS IN THE WORD OF GOD
NOW ALL YOU HAVE TO DO IS
-JUST STAND –

-BY CHARLES LEE SMITH JR.

SOLDIERING SAINTS

SOLIERING SAINTS ARE SAINTS THAT WALK BOLD IN THE LIGHT
SOLDIERING SAINTS ARE SENT OUT TO
CONQUER SPIRITUAL FIGHTS
SOLDIERING SAINTS WALK BY FAITH NOT BY SIGHT
BECAUSE SOLDIERING SAINTS ARE COVERED
BY THE BLOOD OF OUR LORD JESUS CHRIST
AND SOLDIERING SAINTS WALK STRONG IN HIS MIGHT
SOLDIERING SAINTS WALK THROUGH MANY
BATTLES AND MANY STORMS
BECAUSE SOLDIERING SAINTS ARE ROOTED IN THE WORD
AND WEAR THE TRUE ARMOUR FROM THE BLOOD OF THE LORD
SOLDIERING SAINTS, SAINTS WHO ARE CALLED
TO, AND CHOSEN BY THE LORD
SAINTS WHO WON'T FAINT WHEN TEMPTATION IS ABROAD
SOLDIERING SAINTS ARE ALWAYS DOING THAT WHICH IS
PLEASING IN THE SIGHT OF THE LORD,
THAT'S WHY SOLDIERING SAINTS ARE ALWAYS
SENDING UP PRAISE AND GIVING THANKS TO THE LORD
SOLIERING SAINTS YOU MIGHT THINK, ARE ORDINARY PEOPLE
– NOT POSSIBLE –
BECAUSE SOLDIERING SAINTS ARE A HOLY NATION
WHO ALL WALK ON THE SAME FOUNDATION
WE ARE A PECULIAR PEOPLE, CHOSEN
GENERATION AFTER GENERATION
WE ARE THE VOICES IN THE WILDERNESS
THAT SHOUT ABOUT THE COMING OF THE LORD
FOR HE'S COMING NO DOUBT,
SOLDIERING SAINTS PROTECT OUR TEMPLES
WITH ALL OUR THEIR MIGHT
BECAUSE OUR TEMPLES ARE FILLED WITH THE HOLY SPIRIT
WHICH IS THE LIGHT IN OUR LIFE
WE ARE SOLDIERING SAINTS AND THE
HOLY SPIRIT IS WHY WE FIGHT,
SO THAT WE CAN KEEP OUR LIGHT,
THAT'S WHY WE ARE APART OF THE ARMY OF THE LORD
THE MOST GIFTED AND POWERFUL ARMY IN THE WORLD
BECAUSE WE FIGHT NOT WITH STICKS OR STONES
WE FIGHT WITH THE WORD, BECAUSE WITH
THE WORD WE STAND STRONG
SOLIERING SAINTS ARE THE ARMY OF THE LORD

-BY CHARLES LEE SMITH JR.

PRAISE FOR MY MIRACLE

WHEN IM GIVING UP MY PRAISE
ALL EYES ARE AMAZED
BECAUSE THEY DON'T KNOW ABOUT THE SHOW
THE MIRACLE
THAT MY FATHER HAS PERFORMED
RESCUED
SET FREE
RAISED ME UP
NOW THE OLD MAN HAS BECOME NEW
AND MY EYES ARE NOW ABLE TO SEE
MERCY AND GRACE
WHAT A WONDERFUL PLACE TO BE
IN THE HANDS OF THE LORD
TO BE SHAPED AND MOLDED
NOW MY SLEEP IS FULL OF PEACE
AND MY LIFE MADE WITH JOY
THAT'S WHY MY PRAISE ALWAYS AMAZES
THOSE THAT DON'T KNOW ABOUT THE SHOW
MY MIRACLE

-BY CHARLES LEE SMITH JR.

MY HEART WILL KNOW

GIVE ME HOLY EARS
TO HEAR YOUR HOLY VOICE
GIVE ME RIGHTEOUS FEET
TO WALK A RIGHTEOUS PATH
WASH ME WHITE AS SNOW
SO MY HEART WILL KNOW
THAT IT'S YOUR LOVE LORD
THAT I LIVE FOR
IT'S YOUR LOVE THAT KEEPS ME STRONG
EVEN WHEN THE FLESH WANTS TO DO WRONG
IT'S YOUR LOVE THAT SAVED MY LIFE
BECAUSE YOU "LORD"
MADE A GREAT SACRIFICE
YOU GAVE YOUR LIFE THAT I SHOULD LIVE
AND KNOWING SO MY HEART WILL KNOW
THAT IT'S YOUR LOVE LORD
THAT I LIVE FOR

-BY CHARLES LEE SMITH JR.

THE LORDS GOT A HOLD OF ME

THEY DON'T KNOW THAT WHEN I'M
JUMPING FOR JOY, AND SCREAMING
AT THE TOP OF MY VOICE
THAT IT'S BECAUSE "I KNOW"
THE LORDS GOT A HOLD OF ME
HE'S EVERYWHERE I GO
HE'S INVOLVED IN EVERYTHING I DO
SO MANY TIMES HE'S BEEN MY RESCUE
THAT'S WHY THESE DAYS I LOVE HIM TRUE
JUST LIKE ME THERES YOU
SO HUMBLE YOURSELVES BROTHERS AND SISTERS
AND HE'LL BE YOUR RESCUE TOO
IF YOU DIDN'T KNOW NOW YOU KNOW
THAT'S WHAT HE'LL DO, BECAUSE HE'S OUR SAVIOR TOO
HE'S THE SAME YESTERDAY TODAY AND EVERYDAY TO COME
THAT'S WHY I JUMP FOR JOY AND SCREAM
AT THE TOP OF MY VOICE
BECAUSE "I KNOW",
THE LORDS' GOT A HOLD OF ME
WHERE HE IS
IS WHERE I WANT TO BE
LIVING LIFE FREE, JUMPING FOR JOY, AND SCREAMING
AT THE TOP OF MY VOICE
BECAUSE "I KNOW",
THE LORDS GOT A HOLD OF ME

-BY CHARLES LEE SMITH JR.

IF YOU GIVE YOUR LIFE TO THE LORD

IF YOU GIVE YOUR LIFE TO THE LORD
YOU SHOULD LOVE HOW YOU TALK IN THIS
WORLD
IF YOU GIVE YOUR LIFE TO THE LORD
YOU SHOULD LOVE HOW YOU WALK IN THIS
WORLD
IF YOU GIVE YOUR LIFE TO THE LORD
YOU SHOULD LOVE HOW YOU LIVE IN THIS
WORLD
BECAUSE IF YOU GIVE YOUR LIFE TO THE LORD
THEN YOUR LIFE WOULD BE A LIGHT TO THE
WORLD
WHEN YOU GIVE YOUR LIFE TO THE LORD
THERE WON'T BE ONE DAY GOES BY THAT YOU'RE BORED
BECAUSE WE SHOUT AND SING PRAISE TO HIS NAME
AND HE'S TAKEN AWAY THE SHAME
NOW EVERYDAY IS THE SAME
WHEN YOU GIVE YOUR LIFE TO THE LORD
SO GIVE YOUR LIFE TO THE LORD
THEN THE LORD WILL SEE THAT YOU WILL RECEIVE
ALL THOSE FRUITS OF HEAVEN IN YOUR LIFES' REWARDS
SO COME ON GODS CHILDREN LETS GIVE OUR LIFE
TO THE LORD!!

-BY CHARLE LEE SMITH JR.

SAINTS FALL
BUT WE RISE AGAIN

SOME HAVE WONDERED AWAY GONE ASTRAY
DO THINGS SAY THINGS AND FALL FROM GRACE
TEMPTATION HAS TAKEN OVER TEMTATION HAS OVER COME
WE WALK AWAY FROM OUR TALL TOWER
OUR FORTRESS NO LONGER
SURROUNDS US, WE HAVE WALKED AWAY FROM THE PROTECTOR
NOW THE TROUBLE THAT WAS HAS
BECOME TROUBLE THAT'S MORE
MORE THAN BEFORE TROUBLE HAS COME,
NOW UNNUMBERED DAYS
OF FEAR AND TEARS AND WE ASK WHEN OR CAN THIS EVER END
SO WE REMEMBER THE THINGS WE USED
TO DO, WHEN WE STAYED
PRAYED UP AND DID THOSE THINGS THAT WE WAS SUPPOSE TO DO
MEDITATED ON THE WORD DAY AND
NIGHT, THAT KEPT US PREPARED
DAILY FOR OUR SPIRITUAL FIGHTS SO WE
HAVE TO KEEP OUR SIGHTS ON
THE PRIZE AND KEEP THE WORD OF GOD IN OUR HEARTS
AND BEFORE OUR EYES
BECAUSE WE'VE RECEIVED THE SPIRIT OF POWER, LOVE AND A
SOUND MIND
AND THE SPIRIT OF FEAR IS NOT A PART OF
OUR GEAR, SO STAND BACK UP
BROTHERS AND SISTERS AND CALL ON HIS
NAME, BECAUSE HE SAVED YOU ONCE
AND I KNOW HE'LL DO IT AGAIN," JESUS " THAT S HIS NAME

-BY CHARLES LEE SMITH JR.

SAFE IN THE LIGHT

YOU CAN'T TRICK ME NO MORE
BECAUSE MY EYES ARE ON THE LORD
YOU CAN'T MOVE ME NO MORE
BECAUSE IM ROOTED ON HIS WORD
YOU CAN'T USE ME NO MORE
TO DO YOUR' DIRTY WORK
BECAUSE I WORK FOR THE LORD
AND HE'S ALWAYS BY MY SIDE
NOW I MOVE ON HIS STRENGHT
AND WALK BY HIS MIGHT
AND I KNOW EVERYTIME
THE LORD WILL FIGHT MY FIGHTS
AND I KNOW THAT IT'S MINE TO WALK IN HIS LIGHT
SO TAKE YOUR DARKNESS AND BE GONE FROM ME
BECAUSE THE LIGHT I WALK IN
WILL ALWAYS KEEP ME FREE
BECAUSE I WALK BY FAITH NOT BY SIGHT
AND IT WON'T BE ONE DAY
THAT I WON'T HELP HIM FIGHT
BECAUSE I ONCE WAS LOST
BUT NOW I'M FOUND
AND IN HIS LIGHT IS WHERE I WILL ABOUND

-BY CHARLES LEE SMITH JR.

WHEN THE LIGHT COMES ON

WE STARTED AS A CANDLE WE EVOLVED INTO TORCHES
AND BECAME FLAMES ABROAD
NOW ALL GODS CHILDREN CAN SEE THE LIGHT
FROM WAY OFF AND FROM A FAR
NOW WITH THE LIGHT COMES THE WORD
SO WE BECOME BOOKS THAT CAN'T BE BURNED
WE'RE COVERED BY HIS BLOOD PROTECTED BY HIS MIGHT
SO WE STAND AS SOLDIERS PREPARED TO FIGHT
SO WE FIGHT AND WE FIGHT
BUT NOT WITH KNIVES AND GUNS OR STICKS AND STONES
WE FIGHT WITH THE WORD
BECAUSE WITH THE WORD WE STAND STRONG
NOW WITH THE WORD IN OUR HEARTS
THERE'S A BURNING DESIRE
AND WITH THE WORD ON OUR MINDS
OUR HEARTS STAY ON FIRE
NOW IF YOU HAVE EARS TO HEAR, THEN HEAR THE WORD
AND IF YOU HAVE EYES TO SEE THEN FOLLOW JESUS MY LORD
FOR HE'S THE WAY THE TRUTH, AND THE LIFE TO BE
SO JUST LAY YOUR LIFE DOWN
AND HE'LL SET YOU FREE
AND YOU'LL BECOME A CANDLE A TORCH
OR EVEN FLAMES ABROAD
AND THE NEXT GROUP OF CHILDREN
WILL ALSO SEE
WHEN THEIR LIGHTS COME ON

-BY CHARLES LEE SMITH JR.

MUSTARD SEED FAITH

FAITH OF A MUSTARD SEED IS PLANTED INSIDE OF ME
I GOT MUSTARD SEED FAITH ALL OVER ME
AND THE ONLY WAY YOU CAN SEE IT
YOU HAVE TO KNOW JESUS
YOU HAVE TO WALK IN THE WORD SO YOU CAN LIVE IN THE WORD
BECAUSE THE WORD WAS THERE IN THE BEGINNING
AND THE WORD WILL BE THERE IN THE END
' YES ' YOU HAVE TO MAKE THE WORD YOUR BEST FRIEND
THROUGH TIME AND OVER THE YEARS
THAT'S WHEN THAT MUSTARD SEED WILL
HAVE GROWN INTO A TREE
ROOTED DEEP DOWN IN YOU
FROM YOUR HEAD TO YOUR FEET
IT WILL HAVE YOU STANDING TALL AND
EVERYONE WILL HEAR THE BOLDNESS IN YOUR SPEECH
THEY WILL SEE THE WORKS THAT YOU DO
THEN THEY WILL SEE THAT YOU ARE FREE
AND THE WORKS THAT YOU DO WILL BE HOW YOU SPEAK
BECAUSE THE WORKS YOU DO WILL DISPLAY THAT MUSTARD SEED
AND AS TIME GOES ON THEY WILL START TO SEE THE TREE
YOU WON'T HAVE TO SAY ANYTHING
BECAUSE THEY WILL HEAR YOUR HEART SPEAK
THEY WILL HEAR YOUR HEART SAYING
"YEAH, FAITH OF A MUSTARD SEED IS PLANTED INSIDE OF ME"
"I'VE GOT MUSTARD SEED FAITH ALL OVER ME"

-BY CHARLES LEE SMITH JR.
NEW POEM

PRAY LIKE A KID AGAIN

TO MANY NIGHTS I FIND MYSELF ALONE
MY STATE OF MIND, STUCK IN A ZONE
ALL THE TIME TRYING TO GET FREE
BUT MY THOUGHT PROCESS IS STUCK ON FREEZE
AND EACH DAY REPETITIOUSLY I DO THE SAME THING
BUT THE TRUTH IS, TRYING TO KILL THIS FEIGN
BECAUSE EVERY NOW AND AGAIN
I GET A PRAYER IN
AND THEY SAY PRAYER CHANGES THINGS
SO ON MY KNEES AND IT'S THE LORDS NAME
I CALL IT AGAIN AND AGAIN
LIKE CLOCK WORK TRYING TO GET IT IN
IT'S A GOOD THING PRAYING HARD LIKE THIS
ISN'T A SIN
PRAYING WITH SOME SUBSTANCE
PRAYING WITH FAITH STRENGTH
PRAYING TO THE LORD
I HAVE TO PRAY LIKE A KID AGAIN

-BY CHARLES LEE SMITH JR.
NEW POEM

DREAMS FROM THE LORD

DREAMS THEY COME
DREAMS THEY GO
BUT THE DREAMS FROM THE LORD
SHOW US THE WAY TO GO
AND THE WAY YOU KNOW
BECAUSE HE PLANTED IT IN YOUR SOUL

SO FOLLOW YOUR HEART
BECAUSE IT'S YOUR HEART HE KNOWS

A CONNECTION FROM YOUR START
A DIVINE PART OF WHO YOU ARE

SO FOLLOW YOUR HEART
BECAUSE IT'S YOUR HE KNOWS

NOW LISTEN TO YOUR HEART
SO YOUR EYES CAN SEE
AND LISTEN TO YOUR HEART
SO YOUR EARS CAN HEAR
AND NO DOUBT YOU'RE SURE TO BE
IN PLACE CALLED DESTINY
A PLACE WHEN YOU ARRIVE
YOU WILL KNOW THAT YOU'RE FREE

SO FOLLOW YOUR HEART
BECAUSE IT'S YOUR HEART HE KNOWS

-BY CHARLES LEE SMITH JR.
NEW POEM

FATHER SPEAK TO ME

SPEAK TO ME FATHER
TELL ME WHICH WAY TO GO
SPEAK TO ME FATHER
BECAUSE MY FLESHLY EYES ARE CLOSED
DELIVER YOUR STRENGHT UNTO ME
THEN LET YOUR LIGHT CREATE A PATH
THAT MY SPIRIT CAN SEE
PUT YOURSELF IN ME FATHER
SO THAT THE SOLDIER, THE WARRIOR
CAN STAND UP IN ME
ALTHO THE BATTLE IS NOT MINE
THIS IS WAR TIME
BUILD ME UP TO BE A WARRIOR
COVER ME IN THAT PRECIOUS BLOOD
AND I'LL WEAR IT AS MY ARMOUR
THEN I'LL WALK BOLDER
AS A SOLDIER IN THE ARMY
OF THE LORD

-BY CHARLES LEE SMITH JR.
NEW POEM

VICTORY

WHEN I WAKE UP IN THE MORNING
I SEE THE SUN SHINING BRIGHT
I STEP INTO THE NEXT ROOM
AND I SEE MY KIDS FULL OF LIFE
VICTORY IS THERE
SO I GIVE HIM PRAISE AND THANKS
FOR ALL THE GOOD AND BAD HE ALLOWED
IN MY LIFE, MADE ME STRONGER TO ENDURE
MY TRIALS AND STRIFE
NOW EVERY BATTLE SEEMS LIKE A LITTLE FIGHT
BECAUSE VICTORY IS THERE
SO I GIVE HIM PRAISE AND THANKS
FOR ALL HIS LOVE GRACE AND MERCY IN MY LIFE
NOW IM SOLDIERING PREPARED FOR BATTLE
DAY AND NIGHT
SO I TELL THIS STORY SO THE WORLD
CAN SEE HIS LIGHT, AND IF YOU WANT IT
GET ON YOUR KNEE'S AND PRAY TONIGHT
BECAUSE WHEN YOU WAKE UP IN THE MORNING
AND SEE THE SUN SHINING BRIGHT
VICTORY WILL BE THERE
SO GIVE HIM ALL YOUR PRAISE AND THANKS

-BY CHARLES LEE SMITH JR
NEW POEM

LIFE AND DEATH IS IN YOUR TONGUE
"CHOOSE LIFE "

CHOOSE LIFE
CHOOSE YOUR WORDS RIGHT
WE NEED WORDS PEOPLE, WORDS THAT CONQUER STRIFE
WORDS THAT MAKE PEOPLE LAUGH AND NOT FIGHT
WORDS THAT SAY PLEASE AND THANK YOU
WORDS THAT ROLL UP THEIR SLEEVES TO HELP YOU
WORDS THAT ARE LIKE A COOL BREEZE
UNDER GODS BEAUTIFUL TREES
WORDS THAT SAY "I LOVE YOU" AND NOT "I HATE YOU"
WE NEED WORDS PEOPLE
WORDS THAT STOP THE FINGER ON A TRIGGER
WORDS THAT STOP THE WORD NIGGER
WORDS OF POISE, WORDS OF JOY
WORDS WITH A BEAUTIFUL NOISE
WORDS THAT STOP DEATH AND GIVE LIFE
WORDS THAT TALK ABOUT LONG LIFE AND WALKS WITH GOD
WORDS THAT HELP YOUR BROTHER IN NEED
WORDS THAT STOP THE GREEDY AND HELP THE NEEDY
WORDS THAT TRAIN A CHILD IN THE WAY HE'S SUPPOSE TO GO
WORDS THAT HELP KEEP THE TRAINS
ROLLIN' AND THE BOATS AFLOAT
WORDS THAT GIVE SIGHT AND STRENGTHEN YOUR MIGHT
WORDS THAT WIPE AWAY THE TEARS
WORDS THAT CAN END YOUR FEARS
WORDS PEOPLE, WORDS!!
WORDS THAT ARE LIKE A TALL DRINK AND A FULL COURSE MEAL
WORDS THAT ARE LIKE A MEDICAL PILL
WORDS THAT ARE JUST SO REAL, MAN OH MAN REAL WORDS
WORDS THAT DON'T DISTURB BUT WORDS THAT ALERT
WORDS THAT STOP THE WORD CRAKER
WORDS THAT STOP YOU FROM BECOMING SLACKERS
WORDS THAT HELP MOTIVATE, CULTIVATE THE
FUTURE OF OUR NATION UNDER GOD
WORDS THAT ARE COVERED BY THE BLOOD OF CHRIST
WORDS THAT COME FROM GOD SIMPLY TO GIVE LIFE
WORDS THAT ARE NICE
CHOOSE LIFE

-BY CHARLES LEE SMITH JR.
NEW POEM

RUN TO HIM
NO DOUBTS NO HESITATIONS

SOME OF HIS TRUE BLESSINGS
ARE HIS GRACE AND MERCY
SO YOU NEED TO BE RUNNING TO HIM
IN A HURRY
WITH NO DOUBT NO HESITATION
ONCE YOU GET WITH HIM
WATCH THE MANIFESTATION
OF HIS LOVE
FROM DARKNESS TO LIGHT
FROM WRONG TO RIGHT
THERES NO VARIATION OF MODERATION
BECAUSE HIS LOVE IS
FOREVER AND A DAY
FOR ETERNITY
DON'T TRUST ME OR WHAT I SAY
JUST GIVE HIM A CHANCE
NOW YOU SEE HIS MERCY
AND YOU SEE HIS GRACE
KEEP YOUR PRAYERS AND YOUR PRAISE
GOING UP
AND ONE DAY
HOPE YOU GET TO SEE HIS FACE

-BY CHARLES LEE SMITH JR.
NEW POEM

"I AM "

HAD TO RETREAT FROM THE BODY
HAD TO WALK CLOSER TO GOD
SO I COULD BE FREE
HAD TO LET THE SPIRIT
COME IN AND TAKE OVER ME
WALKING IN THE LIGHT DOING THINGS RIGHT

IN MY CLOSET IS WHERE YOU WILL FIND ME
TALKING TO THE FATHER
ASKING HIM TO EXAMINE ME
THEN CLEAN MY TEMPLE OUT
AND MAKE ME A STRONGER ME
ANOINT ME WITH HIS SPIRIT
THEN APPOINT ME TO THAT PREACHING
BEEN SEEING IT IN MY DREAMS
SINCE I WAS A LITTLE ME
GOD SHOWED ME WHO I AM
SO IT'S TIME FOR ME TO BE ME
SO I AM WHO I AM
AND IF YOU ASK ME WHO I AM
I'LL TELL YOU
"I AM"
BECAUSE IN HIS IMAGE AND LIKENESS IM CREATED
SO LIKE HIM
"I AM

-BY CHARLES LEE SMITH JR.
NEW POEM

ALL BECAUSE OF YOU

IT'S NOTHING I DID
OR NOTHING I DO
EVERYTHING I AM
IS ALL BECAUSE OF YOU
HOW YOU TOOK THIS DIRT
AND TURNED INTO CLAY
THEN YOU SHAPED AND MOLDED ME
AND TURNED ME INTO A MASTERPIECE
"YEAH" SOMETHING SPECIAL FOR THE EYES TO SEE
A DIAMOND IN THE ROUGH
WITH YOUR LIGHT SHINING ON ME
NOW IT'S PLAIN FOR THE WHOLE
TO SEE
IT'S ALL ABOUT YOUR GLORY

-BY CHARLES LEE SMITH JR.
NEW POEM

HIS LOVE HIS BLOOD

HIS LOVE IS LONG SUFFERING
HIS LOVE IS UNSTOPPABLE
HIS LOVE IS REMARKABLE, UNCHANGEABLE
NO OTHER LOVE CAN STAND NEXT TO IT
BE COMPARED TO IT
HE'S THE ONLY ONE TO MAKE THAT SACRIFICE

THE LAMB OF GOD

TO GIVE HIS LIFE THE ULTIMATE PRICE
AND BECAUSE OF IT HE'S SAVED MANY LIVES
THROUGH HIS BLOOD I'VE BEEN REDEEMED
NOW HIS BLOOD IT COVERS ME CHANGES ME
KEEPS ME SEEN IN THE EYES OF HIS MAJESTY
JEHOVAH GOD THE ALMIGHTY
THERE'S NO GREATER PLACE TO BE
ALWAYS IN THE PRESENCE OF THE LORD
IS SAFE FOR ME
AND I PRAY IN HIS NAME
THAT'S WHERE I'LL ALWAYS BE
FOR ALL ETERNITY

-BY CHARLES LEE SMITH JR.
NEW POEM

MOTHERS DAY

BONES OF MY BONES
FLESH OF MY FLESH
I THANK THE LORD FOR NOTHING LESS
SHE'S BEAUTIFUL IN EVERYWAY
FROM INWARD TO OUTWARD
IN EVERYTHING SHE DOES, IN EVERYTHING SHE SAYS
SHES BLESSED WITHIN A CURSE BUT BLESSED WITHIN HIS WILL
SHE'S PART OF HIS WORD TO GO AND FILL THE WORLD
SO SHE BRINGS FORTH OUR CHILDREN IN PAIN FROM CONCEPTION
AND IN ALL THE YEARS SHE'S BEEN A TRUE BLESSING
SO BONE OF MY BONES FLESH OF MY FLESH
LOOKING AT YOU I THANK THE LORD FOR NOTHING LESS
SO REMEMBER ALL YOU'VE GONE THROUGH
AND ALL YOU'VE COME THROUGH
AND ALL YOU WILL DO
JUST REMEMBER WHO IT IS
THAT BROUGHT YOU THROUGH
MADE YOU, WHO YOU ARE "JESUS"

WOMAN YOU ARE
MY GRANDMOTHER MY MOTHER MY AUNT
SISTER, DAUGHTER, A COUSIN
OR MY NEIGHBOR, YOU ARE THE MOTHER
OF THE ONE WHO SHED HIS BLOOD
WHICH MADE IT POSSIBLE FOR US TO SHARE HIS ETERNAL LOVE

-BY CHARLES LEE SMITH JR.
NEW POEM

ASK YOURSELF

WHERE WOULD I BE
IF I DIDN'T BELIEVE ON THAT NAME "JESUS"
IF I DIDN'T ASK HIM TO COME LIVE INSIDE ME
IF IT WASN'T FOR THAT GREAT SACRIFICE, HE GAVE HIS LIFE
IF HE DIDN'T PRAY FOR ME TO MAKE A WAY FOR ME
MAN!! THE STRIPES HE TOOK FOR ME

WHERE WOULD I BE
IF I DIDN'T HAVE HIS BLOOD TO COVER ME
HIS LIGHT INSIDE OF ME HIS LOVE TO GUIDE ME

WHERE WOULD I BE
IF MY PAST WASN'T BEHIND ME SLEEP WITHOUT A SOUND
MY FUTURE IN FRONT OF ME A PLIGHT WITH A NEW LIFE
DESTINY THAT'S MEANT FOR ME

WHERE WOULD I BE
IF THE VOICE HE GAVE ME DIDN'T PROPEL
WITH WORDS OF WISDOM
WORDS THAT COULD UNLOCK DOORS TO PRISONS
WORDS THAT COULD CHANGE THE HEART OF A SOUL
WORDS THAT COULD LEAD SOMEONE TO
THE WHOLENESS OF THE LORD
WORDS THAT HELP BRING PEOPLE STRAIGHT OUT OF DARKNESS
WORDS THAT TALK ABOUT THE ONE WE CALL HOLY
THE ONE WHO'S BLOOD THAT COVERS ME
THE ONE WHO'S LIGHT THAT SHINES OVER ME
THE SAME ONE WHO LIVES INSIDE ME
"YEAH "THE ONE WHO GUILDES ME "JESUS "

WHERE WOULD I BE WITHOUT YOU LORD?

NOW ASK YOURSELF
WHERE WOULD YOU BE

-BY CHARLES LEE SMITH JR.
NEW POEM

MY LITTLE SAYINGS

IT IS TIME

FOR ME TO

LIVE MY LIFE

IN A WAY

THAT

"GOD"

WILL BE

GLORIFIED

AT ALL TIMES

-BY CHARLES LEE SMITH JR.

IT'S TIME TO BE CHRIST LIKE

GOD SENT

TO WORSHIP GOD

TO LOVE YOUR BROTHER

TO LOVE YOUR SISTER

TO LOVE YOUR NEIGHBOR

TO EXALT GOD

TO PREACH THE GOSPEL

TO PRAISE GOD

-BY CHARLES LEE SMITH JR.

MEN   YOUR' WIVES

LOVE

WOMAN   YOUR

HUSBANDS

YOUR CHILDREN DEPEND ON IT

-BY CHARLES LEE SMITH JR.

TRUE BREAD FROM HEAVEN

INGREDIENTS:
%100 THE FATHER
%100 THE SON
%100 THE HOLY SPIRIT

ADDED INGRDIENTS:
- A RENEWED MIND
- A RENEWED HEART
- LIFE ETERNAL

-BY CHARLES LEE SMITH JR.

IF YOUR GONNA GOSSIP
LET IT BE THE GOSPEL OF
CHRIST

BECAUSE GOSSIP IS ONLY
GOOD WHEN YOU'RE
TALKING BOUT GREATNESS

-BY CHARLES LEE SMITH JR.

GOSSIP IS ONLY GOOD
WHEN YOU'RE TALKING
ABOUT GREATNESS

SO LET YOUR GOSSIP
BE THE GOSPEL OF
CHRIST

-BY CHARLES LEE SMITH JR.

DONT !

DONT !

CAIN

MURDER

ABLE

YOUR

BROTHER

-BY CHARLES LEE SMITH JR

IF YOU FLOCK WITH

THE RIGHTEOUS

THEN JESUS

IS YOUR SHEPHERD

-BY CHARLES LEE SMITH JR.

LOOING FOR

GOOD WORKERS

OVER AT THE

JESUS IS LORD

FACTORY

-BY CHARLES LEE SMITH JR.

BiG UPS TO

THE TRUTH

JESUS IS

THE WAY

-BY CHARLES LEE SMITH JR.

IF YOU GOT

GOD

THEN YOU GOT

JESUS

THEN IF YOU GOT JESUS

THEN YOU GOT LIFE

AND LIFE ABUNDANTLY

SO LET'S GIVE LIFE BACK

-BY CHARLES LEE SMITH JR.

LORD' LORD JESUS

LORD JESUS- YOU'RE ALWAYS ON MY MIND
LORD JESUS- YOU'RE ALWAYS RIGHT ON TIME
LORD JESUS- YOU'RE THE REASON I SING
LORD JESUS- FOR IT'S YOUR LOVE I REALLY NEED
LORD JESUS- YOU'RE THE BREAD ON WHICH I FEED
LORD JESUS- ON MY KNEES I CALL YOUR NAME
LORD JESUS- EVERYDAY I'LL DO THE SAME
LORD JESUS- FOR YOUR LOVE I SACRIFICE
LORD JESUS- FOR YOUR LOVE I GIVE MY LIFE
LORD JESUS- CAUSE IT'S YOUR LOVE I'LL NEED ALWAY'S
LORD JESUS- IT'S YOUR LOVE THAT KEEPS ME SAFE
LORD JESUS- CAUSE YOUR LOVE IT CLEARS THE WAY

-BY CHARLES LEE SMITH JR.

IF YOU JOIN WITH HIM

TAKING ON ANOTHER DAY
DOING IT MY FATHERS WAY
PRAYING AND I PRAISE HIS NAME
DOING IT EACH DAY THE SAME
HE LIFT ME UP WHEN I WAS DOWN
HE GAVE HIS LOVE AND NOW IM FOUND

-IF YOU JOIN WITH HIM THEN YOU WILL SEE-
THAT HEAVEN IS THE PLACE TO BE

ONE OF THESE DAYS I'LL BE GOING HOME
I'LL BE A PRINCE RIGHT BY HIS THRONE

-IF YOU JOIN WITH HIM THEN YOU WILL SEE -
THAT HEAVEN IS THE PLACE TO BE

SO COME ON SAINTS JUST COME ON IN
CAUSE A LIFE OF SIN WILL BE YOUR END
-IF YOU JOIN WITH HIM THEN YOU WILL SEE -
THAT HEAVEN IS THE PLACE TO BE
HE'LL OPEN YOUR EYES HE'LL GIVE YOU SIGHT
SO YOU CAN SEE WHATS IN THE LIGHT
HE'LL OPEN YOUR EARS SO YOU CAN HEAR
CLEANS YOUR HEART TAKE AWAY YOUR FEARS
WHAT HE DID FOR LAZARUS HE'LL DO FOR YOU
RAISE YOU UP AND SEE YOU THROUGH
SO COME ON SAINTS JUST COME ON IN
CAUSE A LIFE OF SIN WILL BE YOUR END
WE GOTTA PROTECT OUR TEMPLES WITH ALL OUR MIGHT
AND CALL ON THE LORD TO HELP US FIGHT
-SO IF YOU JOIN WITH HIM THEN YOU WILL SEE-
THAT HEAVEN IS THE PLACE TO BE

-BY CHARLES LEE SMIYH JR.

THE GREATEST PLAN

JESUS THE MAN THE FLESH THAT GOD MANIFESTED HIMSELF IN
FOR US TO KNOW LOVE FROM ABOVE
THE HIDDEN SECRET OF THE MOST HIGH
THE GREATEST PLAN,
TO REUNITE THE CREATION OF GOD
BACK INTO HIS HEART
LIKE GEMS AND DIAMONDS BEAUTIFULLY CUT
ALL POLISHED UP, SET OUT FOR DISPLAY SENT OUT TO REPLAY
FOR EACH AND EVERYONE THAT'S CALLED
TO BE RAISED TO HIS STATE OF GRACE
NOW HEAR WE ARE THERE WE GO
SINGING PRAISING AND PREACHING ABOUT THE GREATEST PLAN
THE MAN, "JESUS" THE ONLY BEGOTTEN SON
THE ONLY ONE TO DEFEAT DEATH THE
CROSS THE GRAVE THREE DAYS
A NEW LIFE CREATED
NOW HE'S BEEN RAISED AND SEATED UP HIGH
ON THE RIGHT SIDE OF THE MOST HIGH
NOW ALL EYES LOOK TO THE SKY
WANDERING PONDERING HOW WHERE WHEN
OUR NEW LIFE WILL BEGIN OUR TEMPLES CLEANSED
WASHED FREE OF SIN DEAD IN THE FLESH
TRANSFORMED INTO SPIRITUAL BEINGS
NEW LIFE CREATED UNSEEN WINGS, WE TAKE FLIGHT
TO OUR NEW LIFE FOR OUR NEW HOME THE NEW JERUSALEM
ON NEW STREETS OF GOLD, WHERE ALL THE SAINTS
AND ALL TRANSFORMED CHILDREN WILL LIVE TOGETHER
WITH OUR LOVING FATHER JEHOVAH GOD, AND JESUS OUR LORD
BY OUR SIDE, WHERE WE WILL SEE MAN AND BEAST
BOTH LIVING FREE AND FREE OF FEAR
NO MORE CRYING NO MORE TEARS, EVERYONE WILL BE HAPPY
WITH NOTHING BUT CHEERS AND LOUD PRAISES
THAT WILL GO ON FOR ETERNITY
THERE IT IS THE SECRET THE PLAN FROM
THE BLOOD OF THE LAMB
THE MAN, "JESUS"

-BY CHARLES LEE SMITH JR.

HEAVEN IS THE PLACE TO BE

I USED TO WANT TO BE JODECI OR R-KELLY
YOU KNOW IN THAT INDUSTRY
BUT NOW I WANNA BE FREE LIKE BEBE AND CECE WINANS
KIRK FRANKLIN AND THE FAMILY
PRAISING HIS NAME WITHOUT NO SHAME
I WANNA STAND UP AND SHOUT
KNOWING WITHOUT A DOUBT THAT I CAN BE
WHO I WANNA BE, LIVING FREE IN ECSTACY
A "PRINCE" THAT'S ME
SON OF THE KING, KING OF ALL KINGS
SO I LIVE WITHOUT FEAR ALONG WITH MY PEERS
SONS AND DAUGHTERS OF THE KING
WITH HIS LOVE WE CAN CONQUER ANYTHING
AND WITH OUR LORD BY OUR SIDE WE WON'T MISS A STRIDE
SO WE WALK STRONG IN THE LIGHT PREPARED FOR THE FIGHT
EVERYDAY AND EVERYNIGHT
WE'VE BEEN BLESSED WITH MANY THINGS
AMONG THEM OUR WINGS, NOW WE TAKE FLIGHT FOR THE PLIGHT
INTO THIS PLACE THAT GOD HAS PLANED FOR US
WHERE ECSTACY IS ABUNDANTLY GIVEN IN ALL OUR FANTASIES
WHERE GOD HAS TORN US FROM THE DEAD
SO WE CAN BE BORN AGAIN, NOW OUR FANTASY
CAN NOW BECOME OUR REALITY
"YEAH HEAVEN", HEAVEN IS THE PLACE I WANT TO BE
WHERE ALL THE SAINTS AND ALL GODS CHILDREN
LIVE TOGETHER AS ONE BIG FAMILY
"YEAH HEAVENLY", HEAVEN, THAT'S THE PLACE I WANNA BE

-BY CHARLES LEE SMITH JR.

A PRAYER CAN
CHANGE SOME THINGS

GONE AND SEND YOUR PRAYERS UP
CAUSE THEY SAY PRAYERS CHANGE THINGS
GONE SEND SOME PRAISE TOO
THEN MAYBE HE WILL REARRANGE SOME THINGS
LIKE TAKE YOU FROM THAT DARK PATH
AND PUT YOU IN THAT LIGHT
YOU KNOW, WHERE THE ONLY BEGOTTEN BE
ON THAT PATH THAT'S RIGHT
STRAIGHT AND NARROW
THAT'S WHAT YOU WANT IT TO BE
JUST ENOUGH ROOM
FOR YOU TO GET ON YOUR KNEE'S
SO YOUR PRAYERS CAN GO UP
THEN YOUR BLESSINGS CAN BE RELEASED
EVERYDAY ALL DAY
THAT'S WHAT YOU WANT IT TO BE
A STRAIGHT CONNECTION WITH YOU AND THE MOST HIGH
THAT'S WHY I CONFESS MY LOVE
FOR MY SAVIOR MY CHRIST
CAUSE HE KEEP GIVING NEW CHANCES
AND HE KEEP GIVING ME NEW LIFE
THAT'S WHY IM GONE ROLL WITH HIM TODAY
NAW! IM GONE ROLL WITH HIM FOR LIFE
CAUSE I WANT MY OWN MANSION
UP IN HIS HOUSE
AND I WANT SHARE IN HIS MAJESTIC LIFE

-BY CHARLES LEE SMITH JR.
NEW POEM

SPIRITUAL DANCE

MY EYES ARE CLOSED
MY HEART IS SWOLE
AND MY FEET ARE CARRIED BY WINGS
DON'T KNOW CAN'T SEE THE HEIGHT
BUT I KNOW I'VE TAKEN FLIGHT
TO PLACE OR CITY I'VE NEVER BEEN
AND IN THIS ATMOSPHERE THERE'S NO FEAR
AND HERE IS WHERE PEACE LIVES
JOY IS THE BEST FRIEND AND LOVE HERE NEVER ENDS
OH LORD! IN THIS PLACE I WANT TO LIVE
ALTHOUGH MY EYES ARE CLOSED
THIS PLACE I KNOW
AND THE VOICE HERE IS STRONG
NEVER TALKS JUST SINGS A SONG

YOUR NAME IS HOLY
HOLY IS YOUR NAME

AND IN THIS PLACE THERE'S THIS MAGNIFICANT THRONE
WITH THIS BEAUTIFUL VOICE
SINGING THIS BEAUTIFUL SONG

YOUR NAME IS HOLY
HOLY IS YOUR NAME

-BY CHARLES LEE SMITH JR.
NEW POEM

THE VICTORY IS IN THE BLOOD

IT'S BEEN MANY GOOD BAD AND ROUGH DAYS
IN MY LIFE
BUT HE ALLOWED ME TO GO
THROUGH IT ALL
SO THAT I CAN BECOME A STRONG FIGHTER
A SOLDIER IN THE ARMY OF THE LORD
MESSENGER FOR THE MESSIAH
AND IN EVERY BATTLE
IT SEEMS I WAS BARELY THERE
IT'S ALWAYS BEEN HIM IN MY LIFE
YEAR AFTER YEAR
KEEPING AND PROTECTING ME FROM MY ENEMIES
MAKING SURE NO WEAPONS COULD BE FORMED AGAINST ME
AT THE SAME TIME SHAPING AND MOLDING ME
MAKING SURE I REACH MY DESTINY
THAT PREDESTINED PLAN THAT'S MEANT FOR ME
YEAH! CAUSE I GOT THE MESSIAHS BLOOD ALL OVER ME
THAT BE THE VICTORY

-BY CHARLES LEE SMITH JR.
NEW POEM

"JESUS"
CLAIM THAT NAME

WALKN THROUGH THIS LIFE
I'VE BEEN CALLED ALL KINDS OF THINGS
BUT I CLAIM THE NAME OF JESUS
SO IM WALKING WITH THE KING
BUT THEM AND THEY CALLED HIM NAMES TOO
AMONG OTHER THINGS
AND THEY TRIED TO BRING TO HIM THAT UGLY SHAME
BUT THEY FAILED AT THEIR ON GAME
AND THEY BROUGHT TO THEMSELVES
THAT SAME OLD SHAME

BUT IT'S 2016
AND IM STILL CLAIMING HIS NAME
AND THAT BLOOD – IT'S A GAME CHANGER
AND HIS LOVE – YOU DON'T WANT TO CHANGE IT
HIS NAME – JUST KEEP CLAIMING IT

-BY CHARLES LEE SMITH JR.
NEW POEM

FOREVER
ETERNAL EVERLASTING

PRAISE THE LORD
FOR HIS MERCY ENDURETH FOREVER
AND FOREVER HIS MERCY ENDURETH
SO I HAD TO LINK UP WITH THE LORD
TO GET THAT INSURANCE
LIFE ETERNAL   LIFE EVERLASTING
LIFE WITH LORD
UP IN MY OWN MANSION

-BY CHARLES LE SMITH JR.
NEW POEM

LOOK INSIDE YOURSELF

YOU GOTTA DIG WAY DOWN DEEP INSIDE YOURSELF
FIND GOD IN YOU
AND WHEN YOU DO
TAP HIM ON HIS SHOULDERS
AND TELL HIM TO COME STAND UP
BIG IN YOU
CAUSE THIS A BIG WORLD
WITH BIG PROBLEMS
YOU GONE NEED THEM BIG RESOURCES
IN HELPING YOU SOLVE THEM
SOME OF HIS MERCY SOME OF HIS GRACE
AND YOUR OWN BIG FAITH
TO KEEP YOU STRAIGHT TO KEEP YOU IN THE RIGHT PLACE
WALKN WITH THE SON WALKN IN LOVE
LOVEN ON GODS KIDS AND LOVEN THEM RIGHT
TALKN BOUT THE BROTHERS AND SISTERS
THAT'S IN THE BODY OF CHRIST

-BY CHARLES LEE SMITH JR.

MY LITTLE SAYING

MY GOD IS

AWESOME

FLAWLESS IN ALL

HIS WAYS

SO LIFT YOUR HOLY HANDS

TO HIM

AND KEEP ON PRAYING

-BY CHARLES LEE SMITH JR.

A FRIEND

A FRIEND WILL COMB YOUR HAIR WASH YOUR CLOTHES
AND COOK YOU MEALS
EVEN STAND BY YOU WHILE YOU SAY YOUR PRAYERS

A FRIEND CAN BE ANYONE IN YOUR FAMILY
A FATHER SISTER BROTHER MOST OF ALL YOUR MOTHER
THEY'VE BEEN THERE THROUGH ALL YOUR YOUTH
WATCHED YOU GROW OLDER AND LOVED YOU TRUE
A FRIEND IS SOMEONE WHO KEEPS YOU
SMILING KEEPS YOU LAUGHING
AT THINGS YOU COULDN'T EVEN IMAGINE, HELPS AT TIMES
WHEN LIFE GETS TIGHT, HE'S EVEN THERE
WHEN YOU'RE IN A FIGHT
YOU'VE HAD GOOD TIMES BAD TIMES AND ROUGH ONES TOO
BUT HE'S BEEN THERE ALL ALONG
EVERY TIME YOU FELL HE PICKED YOU UP PAT YOU ON YOUR BACK
AND ENCOURAGED YOU ON
AND WHEN YOU FINALLY GET IT RIGHT, JUST KNOW THAT
HEAVEN IS IN YOUR RIGHTS
SO WHEN IT'S TIME FOR YOU TO GO HOME, HE'S PREPARED
A SEAT IN HEAVEN RIGHT NEXT TO THE THRONE

"A PRINCE THAT'S YOU"
THROUGH THICK AND THIN HE'S ALWAYS BEEN JEHOVAH GOD
YOUR TRUE AND ONLY FRIEND, IF YOU LOOK WITHIN
THEN YOU WILL SEE, IN YOUR OWN SELF, A FRIEND INDEED
JEHOVAH GOD, HE'S IN ALL OF US
THANK YOU JESUS FOR BEING MY FRIEND, WITHOUT YOU
HEAVEN, I COULDN'T GET IN TO MEET MY FATHER JEHOVAH GOD.

-BY CHARLES LEE SMITH JR.

MOVED BY THE SPIRIT

MEDITATION FROM A FREE STATE OF MIND
SPIRITUAL LIT I SPIT ALL THE TIME
OFF THE TIP OF MY TONGUE FROM THE EDGE OF MY MIND
"YEAH" IT'S THE HOLY SPIRIT THAT CAUSES MY THOUGHTS
TO BE SPIRIUALLY DIVINE
BIG TIME FOR THE HEART OF THE SAINTS
BROTHERS AND SISTERS WHO'S SPIRITS IGNITE
WHEN THE FLOW IS RIGHT THE MOOD IS TIGHT
AS WE JAM THE SANCTUARY OUR PRAISES EXPLODE
BLOWING OFF THE ROOF TOP RISES UP TO THE RIGHT SPOT
NOW THE PRESENCE OF THE LORD
HAS COME DOWN WITH US, ALL AROUND US
PURGING US HEALING US MOLDING US LOVING US
SHOWING US THE PATH THAT'S JUST AND JUST FOR US
THE SAINTS WHO TRUST IN HIM AND WALK IN HIS WILL
THE FATHER THE SON THE HOLY SPIRIT YOU ME US WE
WILL ALL BE TOGETHER FOREVER AND A DAY
FOR ETERNITY
IN THE PLACE WHERE THE ANGELS PLAY
AND THEN OUR EYES WILL SEE AND OUR HEARTS WILL KNOW
REAL LOVE REAL PEACE AND REAL JOY
IN THE HOUSE OF THE LORD.

-BY CHARLES LEE SMITH JR.

SPIRITUAL INSPIRATION

IN THE BEAUTIFUL SKY DURING THE DAY I SEE HIS FACE
AT NIGHT AS I GAZE INTO THE STARS
I SEE HIS SMILE BEING FORMED
AND IN MY HEART IT'S VERY WARM
FOR IN MY MIND THAT HELPS CLEARS THE STORM
NOW WHEN IM SLEEP I'M IN HEAVENLY PEACE
FOR I'M WITH MY LORD AND SAVIOR, JESUS.

THEY DON'T KNOW WHAT HE'S DONE
CAUSED A CHANGE AND NOW I'M REBORN
CHANGED MY LIFE ALL INSIDE
TOOK MY SOUL AND MADE IT WHOLE
HE GAVE HIS BLOOD TO PAVE THE WAY
NOW MY PATH IS CLEAR, LONG AND STRAIGHT
ON A ROAD MADE FOR SAINTS.

WE GOTTA BE STRONG CAUSE WE GOTTA GO ON
TO GET TO THE PLACE WHERE THE BLESSINGS ARE STRONG
SO WE GOTTA PUT ASIDE ALL OUR WAYS THAT ARE WRONG
AND TAKE ON THE WAYS OF HIS ADOPTED SONS
GOTTA KEEP OUR EYES OPEN
TO THE THINGS FROM ABOVE
GOTTA KEEP OUR EARS LISTENING,
LISTENING TO THE VOICE WITHIN
BECAUSE, THIS VOICE HELPS KEEPS US FROM SIN

-BY CHARLES LE SMITH JR.

VALENTINES FOR THE
MARRIED SAINTS IN LOVE

WHAT ABOUT A RED ROSE
WHAT ABOUT A BLUE
WHAT ABOUT NEW LOVE
HOW BOUT WE TRY IT
SO LET'S LOOK TO THE LORD
WHOS LOVE IS STRONG FORM
AND LET'S REMEMBER ALL THE REASONS
WHY OUR LOVE HAS REMAINED SEASONED.

HAPPY VALENTINES

WE KNOW A ROSE HAS MANY COLORS
AND VOILETS ARE REALLY BLUE
THE LOVE THAT'S IN MY HEART IS STRENGHTENED DAILY
JUST FOR YOU
FROM THE TIME WE CAME TOGETHER
UNTILL THE DAY OF OUR SALVATION
OUR LOVE WILL LAST THROUGH ANY KIND OF TEMPTATION
BECAUSE WE WALK WITH THE LORD JESUS
WHO IS OUR LOVES' FOUNDATION.

HAPPY VAENTINES

-BY CHARLES LEE SMITH JR.

VALENTINES FOR THE
MARRIED SAINTS IN LOVE

SOME ROSES ARE RED
VOILETS ARE BLUE
AND THE LOVE THAT'S IN MY HEART
I HOLD TRUE FOR YOU
YOU'RE THE APPLE OF MY EYE
THE WOMAN FOR MY LIFE
WITH PATIENCE, SOON BABY YOU WILL BE MY WIFE
I LONG FOR YOUR TOUCH I WANT FOR YOUR LOVE
ONLY THE LORD JESUS CHRIST I PUT ABOVE OUR LOVE
SO PUT YOUR' TRUST IN HIM, AND YOU WILL SEE
THAT NO DOUBT SOON IT WILL BE YOU AND ME
TOGETHER LIVING FREE, LIKE ALWAYS
ECSTASY FROM OUR FANTASIES
MY FAVORITE DREAM

HAPPY VALENTINES

-BY CHARLES LEE SMITH JR.

STEPPIN OUT ON FAITH
STEPPIN OUT TODAY

I'M STEPPIN OUT ON FAITH –I'M STEPPIN OUT TODAY
ON THE WORDS THAT YOU SAID
ON THE PROMISES THAT YOU MADE

SO I'M STEPPIN OUT TODAY – I'M STEPPIN OUT ON FAITH
WITH MY EYES TO THE SKY
MY HANDS HELD HIGH
AND MY VOICE RINGING WIDE

THAT'S WHY I'M STEPPIN OUT TODAY – I'M STEPPIN OUT ON FAITH
THERE WILL BE NO MORE TEARS AND NO MORE FEARS
MY HEART HAS BEEN CHANGED CLEANSED AND REARRANGED
I WILL NEVER BE THE SAME – CAUSE
YOU'VE TAKEN AWAY THE SHAME
YOU ARE THE SUN IN MY DAY
THE MOON IN MY NIGHT
THE LIGHT IN MY LIFE
THAT'S WHY I'M STEPPIN OUT TODAY
CAUSE YOU SHOWED ME THE WAY
THAT'S WHY I'M STEPPIN OUT ON FAITH.

-BY CHARLES LEE SMITH JR.

YOU SHINED YOUR LIGHT ON ME

OH LORD YOU ARE MY EVERYTHING
CAUSE YOU TOOK AND WASHED ME CLEAN
NOW I LIVE TO SING YOU PRAISE
CAUSE YOU SHINED YOUR LIGHT ON ME

YES I DO I LOVE YOUR NAME
THIS IS WHY I STAND AND SING
SINGING PRAISES TO YOUR NAME
SINGING BOUT THE JOY YOU BRING
AND EACH DAY I'LL DO THE SAME
CAUSE YOU SHINED YOUR LIGHT ON ME

NOW I LIVE AND SEE MY DREAMS
SINGING PRAISES TO YOUR NAME
NOW I'M LIVING OUT MY DREAMS
SINGING BOUT THE JOY YOU BRING
YES I DO I LOVE YOUR NAME
CAUSE YOU ARE MY EVERY THING
THIS IS WHY I STAND AND SING
ALL MY PRAISES UP TO YOU.

-BY CHARLES LEE SMITH JR.

Printed in the United States
By Bookmasters